THE SECRETS OF...

MONEY MANAGEMENT

Manage Your Money Like The Riches

Written by Senol Asan,

AlterHabit Institute, Delaware

THE SECRETS OF...

MONEY MANAGEMENT

© 2012 Senol Asan, AlterHabit Institute

"My problem lies in reconciling my gross habits with my net income."

Errol Flynn – American actor (1909 – 1959)

"The philosophy of the rich and the poor is this: the rich invest their money and spend what is left. The poor spend their money and invest what is left."

Robert Kiyosaki - American investor, businessman, self-help author, motivational speaker (born in 1947)

"Why is there so much month left at the end of the money?"

Anonymous

AKNOWLEDGEMENT

My Most Grateful Thanks:

- To all those who had the ability to develop my curiosity - **all the teachers** in the formative years;

- To all those who had enough patience with me to stand and repeat until I learned what I had to learn - **all my colleagues** throughout my entire career;

- To all those who showed me how to manage my money and, more importantly, which are principles that I have to follow in order to establish and maintain a certain standard - **all my clients**;

- To all those who have shared their knowledge, directly or through books and recorded materials - **all my mentors**;

- **To my beloved family** for being always by my side and supporting me wholeheartedly in all my endeavors.

DEDICATION

To my one and only love,

Thank you for being in my life

WARNING

All information provided is of the highest quality. All the methods presented were tested in practice by the most financially successful customers I have met in my banking career.

Use of this book WILL PROVIDE maximum results only to the extent the information is assimilated, internalized, and implemented EVERY DAY.

Unfortunately, the author and nor other collaborators have not found a method that brings results without requiring the active involvement of the reader.

This manual is an INVESTMENT only to the extent that information in it is applied; otherwise it is an EXPENSE of time and resources which the author advises you NOT TO DO.

Before taking a decision on your situation, you should check a professional financial and/or legal counselor, as there is suggested many times in the book.

TABLE OF CONTENTS

Money Management

Money Management

INTRODUCTION

I am no writer. I started my career as a banker. In fact, most of my life I was involved in retail banking and I had the opportunity to learn from my customers by seeing what the successful ones were doing. In the same time, I had the chance to get an idea about what to avoid from my less wealthy customers.

Unlike any other books on money management and personal finance, I will take a much more effective approach to financial planning and personal budgeting. The practice of money management, even it sounds pretentious, should be a straightforward, life-enabling, and user friendly way to organize, create, and manage your fortune. In the same time, money management should be motivating enough to build better habits regarding how you use your money.

On the other hand, when you look to what happens in reality, it becomes clear that an extremely small number of people are actually using a money management system or tool. Most people are caught in a vicious circle. They start learning about managing their finances, at some extent even try some of the principles in their life, and they end-up by going back to their old habits. Their opinion is that money management and personal budgeting does not work for their circumstances.

Some people will appreciate budgeting and money management as an unnecessary burden and an effective way to remove all the comfort and enjoyment from their life.

Other will say that they are well disciplined about their money, and they can stop their unnecessary spending if and when they want.

And yet, you will see both types going down and down on the road to financial trouble, getting deeper and deeper in debt, and, in some cases, they get to the state to declare bankruptcy.

In the present guide, The Secrets of Money Management, I will show you how to set up better a way to manage your money, stick to your plans and enjoy the success.

You will find that, by the time you will learn how to have a monthly surplus to yourself and how to start building your wealth step-by-step. You will become more knowledgeable about your spending and spending habits and you will learn how to start saving. You will learn to change your thinking patterns related to money and spending and you will develop a wealth attitude.

Money Management

Money management is the only means of success in wealth creation and it is only source for changing your behaviors related to wealth and riches.

Did you ever felt that month is too long for your income? Did you ever experience the situation to run out of cash before running out of the month? Did you notice how your bills seem to grow faster than your income?

This is the reality call: stop spending and start investing! If you choose to spend, it is gone forever. If you choose to invest, it will bring you more.

In this simple guide, you will start learning what the difference between spending and investing is. When I say investing it is not only about stocks and bonds and investment funds. You may choose to invest in yourself by enrolling to a training program. You may choose to invest by renting a different home in a better neighborhood. Investing is more than you probably believe at this time.

How about your retirement? Did you ever thought how your retirement years will look like? How about planting the seed for the tree that will lay its shadow where you will rest after retiring right now? One proverb says: "the best time to plant a tree is twenty years ago; the next best time is now".

You will find some simple and yet powerful methods on how to create, plan, revise and improve, implement, and stick to the budget that will ensure your future. You will notice that money management is a process, and you will learn how to master its dynamics and your personal budget will become the barometer of you financial health and future prosperity.

What's in it for you?

When most of the people think about money management and budgeting, they start thinking on how a budget will show them what they cannot afford.

Money management seems to turn into an unpleasant concept due to the restrictions that it seems to bring in your life. You may perceive that planning your spending, budgeting and sticking to the plan will limit your comfort and/or will take out indulging in our days temptations out of your life.

Reality is that money management is more about focusing your attention and energy on finding ways to stretch and spend your income wiser. In simple word, successful money management is finding ways to make your money going further instead of going forever.

This simple how-to guide was created to help you setting up your own personal money management system, your personal budget, and helping you create the present and future you want!

Money Management

You will find some general money-saving tips; you will also find some investing tips in the coming pages. Yet, the main thing you should focus when you read and learn about the concepts in this guide are the mindset and spending patterns that you need to develop to become financially successful.

You may realize that there are some attitudes, habits and spending patterns that we need to become aware about, asses and even change, before starting your money management process.

For most people, a personal budget means only a spending plan. In fact, for a spending plan you need only a journal and a pen. Any well-kept journal can show you where your money went.

For some people, money management is about fitting their spending to their income. It reflects what they can and cannot afford and how to plan their spending in order to keep the expenses in their means every month. In some of these cases, it becomes even a habit to making a personal budget they can live and stick to it.

One of the goals of the book is to reveal the secrets of money management and highlight a simple, powerful, and systematic process to setting up a successful budget as a tool to improve the quality of your life.

"Manage Your Money Like The Riches", is a simple how-to guide created to take you through the entire process and help you answer who, why, when, what, where and how questions related to financial planning.

Yet, the main focus of the book is to focus your attention and energy to the true objective of managing your money. Money management is not to be used to restrict spending and keep living a cheap life. The main objective is to provide you insights, informed decisions, actions and sustained discipline regarding your personal financials and your future wealth.

The Secrets of Money Management will give you the secret concepts that will help you have a systematic approach to managing your wealth. It focuses on everyday secrets used by the successful people and focuses on applying these "best practices" in your own life.

How to use this book

When people get new information, they usually tend to compare it and analyze it through their own experience and filters and decide upon its usefulness.

If the information is in line with what they know, people tend to believe it as being true and take it for granted.

If there is something that is contrary to what they know, their first impulse is to deny it and to find reasons why the information is wrong or not applicable in their situation.

Money Management

You will find in this material some information which you will say its common sense and rather basic. In the same time, you may find other information that will be totally out of the way you are used to think now.

In order to get the maximum from this book, I invite you to read it first time without any judgment on the information. Read it as a story, a fantasy or a science-fiction book. Just get a glimpse on a different point of view and don't think if it is right or wrong.

The second time, I would ask you to read it as a training book. Take time to think about your personal situation and apply the tips and methods presented in your daily routine.

Some of the methods in this book might apply to your particular circumstance, and others may be out of the practical application at all.

You will find ideas, tips, process stages, and practical savings and investing suggestions that you may not noticed until now.

All the information is about general principles and should be assessed on an individual basis. When making decisions that could affect your financial present or future, you need to consider professional help from a financial advisor who knows your case

REMEMBER: *The way you think now got you in your current situation. If you want to change something in your current situation, you have to make some changes in your current routines.*

WHAT IS MONEY MANAGEMENT?

For most people, a money management is just a simplistic process to balance the inflow of money with the outflow. In other words: income is what comes in and expenses are what move out! It is a one-way cash management process.

After a period of struggling with this attitude and behavior regarding personal budgeting, these people find themselves in the same place where they started the process.

For most people, income is somewhat fixed to their salary and the spending usually increases over time as the needs change. Getting a loan or at least a credit card is also something most people are used to do nowadays. If it starts to sound like a never ending struggle, yes it is. Most people find themselves caught in the trap of increasing needs and more or less constant income. It becomes a lifetime battle to get financial freedom they dream.

A real money management approach may be the solution. The systemic approach to managing money and the awareness about the secret principles of setting-up a successful personal budget are the keys to wealth.

Money management is a structured process and planning activity, dealing with personal financial resources and context. It is a proactive, hands-on approach, focused, technical and disciplined strategy to getting a handle on the current financial situation in your life.

It concerns setting realistically, S.M.A.R.T. financial goals for the household, sticking to it, celebrating successes, learning from failures and trying again if you do not succeed or get it right the first time round. It is about shifting focus completely from an overall spending focus to an investing and savings orientation.

Who should manage money?

Every personal situation is unique and distinct. There cannot be a one-size-fits-all plan and approach that works for everyone.

There are tremendously different situations: fixed salary income, commission based incomes, part-time job incomes, home based business incomes, debt-ridden or bankruptcy situations, state subsidized situation and various others. Money management is valuable and different for every single case.

All financial advisors talk about rewarding yourself for developing and maintaining financial responsibility, discipline and habits, to increase your motivation and success levels.

Understanding and applying money management principles is the first step. Planning and sticking to a budget may seem at first something pretty hard to do. Repeating and continuous feeling of the benefits of a good budgeting cycle and seeing the evolution in your life has to keep the motivation going.

Financial awareness, proper money management, savings and investments, planning the retirement, financial goals, active and hands-on approach to personal financial aspect of existence, is becoming more and more important for the financial survival and well-being everywhere and everyone.

Why to manage your money?

Here are top ten reasons to have a start managing your money consciously and systematically:

1. Money management is your vehicle. It can be a very powerful tool on your journey to financial success. It will take you on your route to your financial goals. It leads you and gives you insights how you should change from spending to investing and provides you good financial management, balance and responsibility. You may desire financial freedom or you may have dreams about your financial situation, but if you do plan

reaching them and you do not keep track on your evolution, you may end up far away from your goals.

2.   A money management system is a control facilitator. A money management system gives you the power to control your money. It helps deal with the financial pressure and to start controlling your financial life.

3.   A budget as the main tool of money management system is the true image of your current situation and financial means. A budget helps you in keeping your living within your real means and in finding solutions to wiser spending.

4.   Money management helps you achieve your financial related goals. It consists of a mechanism for laying down the foundation for future savings and investments.

5.   Sticking to a realistic budget gives you hints to free up cash so you can spend your money wiser. It helps you focus your spending on things that are really important instead of wasting your income.

6.   A money management approach helps you to keep the focus on medium and long term goals. Having a plan and a personal budget reveals aspects where you are habitually spending too much and gives you solutions to refocus on your goals.

7.   Money management prepares you for emergencies or unanticipated expenses that might appear in your life. Having this kind of aspects covered it gives you're the peace of mind to

focus your attention to what you want instead of worrying about what might get wrong.

8.   Money management can improve your relationships. A good way to manage your money is more than a spending plan. Creating and maintaining good relationships may need some financial investments beyond time investment. Planned properly, a money management tool will offer solutions to your investments in relationships. In your personal relationships it can be also a great communication tool that will tell your partner about common dreams and efforts needed to achieve financial objectives.

9.   A money management system keeps you out of debt by giving you the limits of your means. In the same time, it is the single and perfect tool to get out of debt faster and easier by delivering solutions to free up some cash to make the extra payments on your installments.

10. Managing your money reduces stress and gives you better sleep. Done realistic and in the right manner take off the financial pressure that you may face when you have to keep focusing on how to make ends meet.

REMEMBER*: Having a good money management system is like having a supercar with GPS on your trip in a foreign country.*

Money Management

What are the main elements of money management?

At this point you may be thinking what the main elements of a good money management tool are.

At its basics, a money management tool consists of two main categories:

1.   Inflow of cash (income from salary, commissions, bonuses, interest from savings, part-time job income, etc.)

2.   Outflow of cash (expenses)

The inflow of cash is commonly easy to address. You probably are very aware of the main sources of your money.

In the most cases, the outflow of money is the main reason of financial pressure and trouble. We all have some habitual expenses, some spending habits that we are not aware about. Think for a moment about the small things you usually do not pay attention.

When I made this experiment for myself, I realized that I was spending more than 300$ every month without being aware. I become aware about my daily coffee routine. On my way to the office I always stopped to a coffee shop and too a big black Americano for more than 2$. In simple words a big simple coffee; no sugar, no milk. In simple words I was spending about 50$ every month on a simple coffee that I could make myself in the office with less than half of the money. The same case was with the parking payments and newspapers. I was paying a lot of money on parking space when my office was less than 25 minutes walking distance from my home and I was spending on newspapers that I could read for free on the internet.

How about your own spending habits that you are not aware about?

In budgeting exercise as part of money management system, putting expense items into big clusters or categories is a helpful method. This offers a better control on the present situation and provides a good reality check when you decide to start your journey towards your financial goals.

Some of the main clusters should be:

- Monthly dues or obligations – you may include in this cluster all the external bills that you have to pay: mortgage/rent, insurance (health, auto, home, life), professional fees and dues, tuition or day care for the kids (if case), loans (bank fees and interest), taxes (state, property, etc.), and all other dues you may face to keep your living standards.

- Necessities – here you should include things that you really need to survive: food, groceries, utilities (gas, water, electric, garbage, and sewer); household supplies, personal hygiene products, etc.

Money Management

- Daily expenses – you should keep track on your spending habits you are not aware about: lunch at work, drinks (snacks, sodas, coffee, etc.), parking fees, tolls, newspapers, and all other habitual spending that you may have; a simple solution to become aware of this kind of spending is to write in a small notebook every time you put your hand in your pocket to pay something regardless if it is cash or card payment;

- Relationship Investments – these would be relationship required expenses: parties, weddings, official and informal events, relationship related entertainment (weekend outing, movies, concerts, other entertainment), dining out and all other type of expenses related to developing and keeping relationships, both business and personal

- Personal expenses – hobbies, recreation, parties and going out, personal care, personal gifts (CD's, clothes, shoes, jewelry, etc.)

- Personal Investments – books, training courses, schooling, etc.

- Charity – contributions, donations, and other related items.

- Saving and Investing — retirement plans, pension funds, investment projects, savings accounts and all the other related items

REMEMBER: *In a simple and basic way money management is optimizing your inflow and out flow of money.*

Final thoughts on what money management is

Become your own expert and focus on coming up with new ideas about how to save and invest in your future, budget better, and spend wiser! Your strategies should rise from a deep knowledge of your particular situation, wants, needs, and desires. Discover which tips and ideas work for your case. After all, personal well-being has a personal, tailored and unique definition for each and every one of us.

A well thought out, planned and realistic way to manage your money will serve as a car with a GPS system incorporated to get you there. It is a financial tool facilitating your financial dreams, goals and aspirations, making them a reality. Money management will enable you to reach your financial targets and set goals.

REMEMBER: *Managing your money appropriately is your most important step on your journey to financial*

success.

YOUR OWN MONEY MANAGEMENT SYSTEM

Starting to manage your money consciously may seem a little bit scary and may look like a hard endeavor. A good place to start is right here, right now. You may start with an objective assessment of your current financial situation.

Start assessing where you really are in your financial life. You may think you know and yet you should make this assessment really deep. Take the time to list, study and analyze you financial situation. Become aware of your present financial worth, define your financial goals, and set a plan and a deadline for each of them. Where and how do you start?

What is your financial worth now?

The principle is simple: before you start your journey to your financial goals, you have to know where you start from and what it may take you to complete the journey.

Money Management

A starting point in assessing you current situation may be studying your bank statements, tax return, and the most recent credit report.

Think and list all your sources of income, regular, temporary or seasonal, part-time job income, and bonuses that you might have. Answer to the following questions: What is your total income? How are you receiving the income (monthly, weekly, etc.)? Are all the income sources generating with the same regularity?

Depending on your answers you need to start to manage your money accordingly. In some cases you may choose to let some of the income sources out of your plans. If the bonuses or part-time incomes are not regular and you cannot forecast them, it would be better to budget without them and when they appear to use them to make extra payments on your debts or save them entirely.

Focus on your assets. Consider all banking accounts, savings, saving union accounts, money and capital market accounts, certificates of deposit. List all the assets that can be quickly turned into money.

Think about consolidating accounts if you realize that you have many accounts spread out on multiple banks and reduce your banking fees. This maneuver will also help you improve tracking of your spending.

Other assets you should consider might include valuables like: jewelry and watches, collectables of any kind, art (paintings, sculptures, etc.), antiques (furniture, books, watches) and many more.

You should list also real-estate properties and other type of properties that may be turned into money is you will face a very serious situation.

In most cases, this step is really revelatory. You may realize that your situation is not as hard as you feel about it and you have some sources of cash like assets in hand if needed.

Now that you have a quite good look about your assets side, let's think about your liabilities. What and to whom do you owe?

List all your debt including banking loans, credit cards, leasing, mortgages, money borrowed from friends and family, advance cash received from employer of clients and all other type of possible debts you may have.

You have a pretty clear picture about your financial net worth at this moment. The difference between all your assets and all your liabilities gives you your financial net value at this moment.

You may realize that even having a lot of debt your net value is still positive and your financial situation is better that you knew.

In some cases, you may realize that your financial situation is not as good as expected and you should definitely change something immediately.

Money Management

Either way you know where your financial journey starts. It is the time to start budgeting journey and to make the changes in your life.

Some of the books published on the subject of money management center around how to get debt free, stay out of debt and live a prosperous life. Some of them suggest frugal living is the key to long term financial goal achievement. You may find a lot of examples promoting the cheapskate living and a monthly makeover that focuses on cutting off expenses and living within your present means.

A paradigm-shift is required be able to create successful money management system. The most important secret is to change your mindset from a short term perspective about money to a long term one. Start creating a long-range view and a long term thinking pattern when it comes to your financial life.

Start small and with discipline, commitment and steady pace, optimizing financial behaviors on the way, you will be able to plan, implement and follow a personal budget that will lead you to your financial future you want.

REMEMBER: *Your present situation is only the starting point towards your financial dream.*

How to start managing your money?

You decided to start this journey and now you have to take the second step on managing your money process.

How to start planning and managing money? Here are some general aspects and methods you will find helpful in assisting you to start your budget and improve your money management skills on the way:

- The first and foremost significant step that I mentioned earlier is changing your thinking patterns about money management; managing your money is not a monthly event; it is a day-to-day process; you have to be aware of implementation and evolution of your personal financial plan every single moment;

- The second mind change you have to make is about financial planning range; focus on medium and long term needs and goals; create a longer range vision about your financial situation;

- The third shift you have to make is about your attitude toward spending; start focusing on investing; analyze all you expenses from the return point of view; do this expense returns something on the long term or is just money gone forever;

- The fourth step you should consider is about developing an awareness of how and what you earn, handle, save and spend or invest; keep a clear record about all your inflows and outflows of money regardless of their size; sometimes the smallest but habitual and daily things will make the biggest difference between financial success and financial trouble; understand you income and spending; analyze income cycle for one year and be aware about your spending habits

- The fifth major change you have to make is about getting out of the most common game in nowadays: "Keeping-up with the Jones's"; start focusing on your own goals and dreams regarding the financial life you want;

- Set your own financial and budget goals; think on what makes you tick and set goals that will motivate you on the way;

- Stop impulse driven purchases; you may start to realize that you have a lot of expenses due to impulse driven purchases; learn how to delay a purchase

- Set clear spending limits and keep them no matter what;

- Set up automated savings and spending mechanisms; almost all the banks have standing order services that will allow you to set a monthly amount to a savings account

- Plan your obligations and must pay – smooth out large size bills with reserve accounts

- Plan your necessities and look for ways to economize

- Celebrate regularly when you see your financial situation and your money management skills improving; indulge a little and reward yourself; you may consider even nonfinancial rewards

These are the starting points to saving money, planning ahead and driving for money management success!

REMEMBER: *Before changing your financial life you should change yourself. Mindset, thinking patterns, attitude and long term vision are the key to a successful money management system.*

Traps in money management

Some people take the decision and start considering money management. They are really convinced about the importance of managing their money actively. Some of them even start and learn a lot about personal and business budgeting, they put a lot of effort in the budgeting process, but at some point something happens, they give up, and they end up right where they started.

There are four major causes of money management failure. Being aware about these traps is your most powerful tool to create a successful money management habit.

Trap #1 – Wrong Mindset and Perspective

The biggest trap in managing your money is the wrong mindset.

If you start asking people about money management most of them, they will tell you that it is a monthly planning process to spend the money. Some of them will tell you that managing your money is the way that helps you make ends meet. And most of them will look at money management as a regular event instead as a day-to-day habit.

Managing money is more than a record of expenses or a balance of inflow and outflow. It is your vehicle and a roadmap on your financial journey. It provides you valuable information and even solutions to optimize your expenses and teaches you to think in investment terms.

Trap #2 – Wrong Attitude

The importance of the right attitude cannot be highlighted enough. Having a positive attitude about money management is vital to your success. If you look on managing money in negative terms (such as cost cutting procedure, financial dieting, limiting your pleasures, a sacrifice, etc.), you are on your way to fail.

As I pointed out earlier, money management is a process that should be part of your financial life every single moment.

Unless you change your attitude towards it, you will have a very hard time to embed it in your daily life.

Start creating a positive attitude towards money management. Think about it as a vehicle and a tool to achieve your dreams and to objectives. Postponing insignificant pleasures given by instant and impulse spending will worth the effort to achieve your financial dreams.

Trap #3 - Lack of Motivation

Why do you even bother managing your money? Is your money management effort supported by external or internal motivators? Some of the external motivators could be a debt repayment plan agreed with a collection or financial counseling agency, a bankruptcy agreement or other external pressures that you may face. These kinds of motivators are very good to make you start budgeting, but in time, they will fade out and will not be the real kind of support you need to create your money management habit. Do you really and deeply believe that actively managing your money will lead you to your dreams and goals? If the answer is yes, probably you are already on the right direction. The best motivators are the internal ones and the deep desire to achieve your dreams.

When you feel like in need of help in the motivation, take a tour on "Why to manage your money" and have a dose of it.

Trap # 4 - Unrealistic Expectations

What are your expectations from money management experience? Are you thinking that having a plan and applying it will instantly turn your financial situation? Are you expecting that money management will shift yearlong habits in a matter of weeks or months? Do you think that following a budget will turn you immediately into a modern Midas and everything you touch will turn into money?

I have to stress again that money management is a process and it should be embedded into your day-to-day life. This will take some time and some effort. In the same time, managing your money is a dynamic process. You have to make adjustments constantly to optimize your inflow and outflow dependent on the evolution of your needs and goals. Money management is an endurance process. You have to stick to it and focus and the progress you make every single day. In the end the rewards will be achieving all your financial dreams and goals.

REMEMBER: *Starting to actively manage your money without having the right mindset, perspective, and attitude, internal motivation, and realistic expectations, it is the surest way to go straight to financial failure.*

You have to be sure to rule out these four traps even before you begin the process in order to set the right bases to create a successful personal budget.

Define your financial goals

One sure way to rule out the four traps of budgeting is to set your financial goals even before you start the process of managing your money.

Everyone has a wish list. Every one of us has some goals and some objectives. And in nowadays most of our dreams and desires tend to relate to our financial health.

In the same time, you will always find things and ways to spend your earnings. One of the most common mistakes people tend to make is the silly game of "Keeping-up with the Jones's".

You are different now. Take your time and list the most important dreams and goals for your life. Think about what you want to be. Answer to one question: "What would you be/do/have if money wouldn't be an issue?" Take all the time you need to define your ideal life. Think about every aspect of it without considering your current financial situation.

After you have a clear picture about how you would like your life to look like, take a short break. Drink a glass of water, take a 10 minutes' walk, do anything that will take your conscious mind

Money Management

from the previous task. Now is the time to start defining your financial situation that you need to achieve your dream life. Stop thinking on your present financial situation and start focusing on how you want it to be.

You most probably picture a totally different situation. In my case, I was far away from my ideal financial vision. When I say far away I mean really far. I was over 200.000$ in debt, and my financial net worth was less than 10.000$.

If your picture is also really far from your present situation, start breaking down the long term goal into small goals. Remember that money management is a lifelong process and you need a long-range perspective about your financial health.

You may think about splitting your goal into smaller objectives with ongoing investments. You may need to consider some training costs to develop yourself in order to increase your income. You may think about small monthly extra payments on your debts. You may think about small savings each month to start a home based business as a part-time income generator.

Take the time to make a roadmap from your present situation to your ideal financial life marked with small, realistic and achievable milestones. Even if now it seems very hard, you may star with some small steps and keep going. Do not worry. I highlight again: managing your money is a long-term and dynamic process.

Money Management

As you will go on the road you will start to see new milestones and you will be able to reach out further and further.

You may choose to do this exercise regularly to keep track on the development of your dreams and your evolution on the journey to achieve them.

REMEMBER: *Keep your focus on your dreams to keep you on the right direction and to remind you why you are doing all the money management process and efforts.*

Money Management

MONEY MANAGEMENT PROCESS

Here you are now! You know your starting point, you know your destination, you have some of the milestones, and you are ready to start actively managing your money.

In order to start the process you have to take the simple five basic steps:

- <u>Step one:</u>   Understand your money inflow

- <u>Step two:</u>   Understand your expenses

- <u>Step three:</u>   Understand your spending habits

- <u>Step four:</u>   Balance your budget.

- <u>Step five:</u>   Optimize your money management.

You may think that it is too simple and too common sense. How come so many people are not doing it, and even if they do it a lot of them fail?

However, that is all about the starting a money management process. Let's look closer to these steps and find out the secrets of the great achievers use.

Step 1: Understand your money inflow

Your money inflow consists of the total amount of money that enters into your life. Usually when you think about the money inflow you resume yourself to your regular income regardless if it is a fixed salary or commission based income or any other type of payment you may receive.

Managing your money successfully is based on understanding your total money inflow. Think about all amounts that you get. List all sources of money that you have at this moment: salary, commissions, part-time activities income, dividends, interest from savings, alimony, state subsidies, etc. Make a really comprehensive list of all sources of income regardless of their size or regularity.

Now, start putting near every type of income the amount that it generates and the regularity. You will find that you have some income sources that generate money on monthly bases, some on others quarterly, and others have no regularity. Based on these insights you can make a forecast regarding your monthly income for almost an entire year. If you have some sources of income that you are not sure about take them out from your forecast. For example, if you expect some money or gift certificates for your birthday and you are not sure about the amount you may choose not to put them into the inflow.

Look and analyze the money inflow variations during the year and get a good overview what are the main contributors to these variations. What is the seasonality of your income? How your money sources vary over each month? Are there any ways to you can make these variations smaller? Get a grasp about your minimum monthly income you have to meet when making your expenses.

Step 2: Understand your expenses

Now that you have a clear picture about your money inflow, it is time to think about outflow of money. This can be a little bit difficult to do. Definitely you can think and list all the high ticket payments you may face. Usually the small ticket but high frequency expenses are the one that gives you most of the problems.

Here are some of the most common expenses that people lists when then start budgeting:

- Necessities like food and utilities expenses (gas, electricity, water, phone, sewage)
- Clothes, shoes, laundry, dry-cleaning
- Transportation: gas, parking, car repair, tolls, car taxes, public transportation fares
- Housing expenses: rent, mortgages, property taxes, house repair, furniture, small items for home, cleaning supplies, gardener and/or housekeeper,

Money Management

- Medical expenses: doctor, dentist, medicine, hospital or clinic.

- Savings: a future purchase, emergency or buffer funds, retirement plans, investments.

- Installment payments: car, furniture, charge accounts, credit card accounts, loans.

- Pocket money: tobacco, drinks, coffee, sodas, newspapers, magazines, etc.

- Entertainment and Recreation expenses: movies, theatre, opera, eating out, sports and equipment, club membership, cable TV, renting multimedia, vacation, mailing

- Personal investments: schooling bills, books, workshops, training courses, lessons, conferences and more.

- Donations: charitable donations, religious giving (church, synagogue, mosque, temple, etc.), and other types of gifts

- Insurance: life, health, house, car and property

- Taxes: if not deducted from your pay check (income, social security, state tax, etc.)

How does your list look like? How many of these types of expenses to you have? Are there any other expenses you should put on the list?

Step 3: Understand your spending and spending habits

Here we are on the step 3 which is probably the hard part of managing your money process. Now you have to put some effort to record the most accurate information about your spending.

Here are some categories and estimates about your actual spending you may encounter during a regular month. You should use them as a guideline before you start to track your own actual spending:

- <u>Monthly expenses that stay the same (fix expenses)</u> – car, rental, mortgage, loan, insurance, cable TV (except pay-per-view), internet, and other type of payments

- <u>Monthly expenses that may vary (variable expenses)</u> – utilities (gas and heating, electricity, phones, sewage, etc.), and more. Take time to add up costs for the last six months or, even better, one entire year and divide by six or twelve to calculate a good estimate on your monthly average costs.

- <u>Quarterly or bi-annual expenses (regular expenses)</u> – insurances, taxes, etc.

- <u>Annual expenses (regular expenses)</u> – birthday and anniversary gifts, insurances, taxes, etc.

- <u>Unexpected expenses (extraordinary expenses)</u> – there are sometimes events that occur to your life without any heads-up notice; you should be prepared with an emergency or contingency fund; what you can afford to set aside as a buffer or emergency, contingency fund; in recent financial literature the experts say the you should have a six to nine month income into your reserves.

You have a good estimate on your regular payments and your regular payment variation during an entire year.

Here comes the hard part I was mentioning earlier. The expenses that occur more than once a month like food, gas, entertainment, recreation. This is type of expenses that are usually small ticket size expenses that can turn your financial situation upside-down.

The simplest way to keep an accurate record on this apparently "black hole" of your cash is to invest in a small note book and in a pen. You should carry these important money management tools with you all the time for at least a month. Keep writing down all the money that is leaving your pocket or bank account. You should write down the smallest payment you make. For example, giving some change to a bagger on the street should find its place in your note book.

You may consider the above example a little bit too far. It may seem this way, but it will help you keep track on your other spending habits you are not aware. Do you take a coffee on your way to the office every morning as I used to do? Are you using your car and pay for the parking place even when you have to travel in walking distance? These are types of habits that you are not aware about and, when you add up for an entire year, it costs you a lot of money that you can use to achieve your dreams faster.

Step 4: Balance your budget

Compare your total expenses with your real inflow of cash. There can be one of the following scenarios:

Neutral result: Inflow of cash is equal to outflow – you are so good at spending that you are able to spend all your money but not more that you have; it's a good situation if your spending contains some investments in yourself and in your future; personal finance gurus and money management literature state that you have to have at least 10% of your inflow directed to some kind of savings or investments plan and other 10% in personal investments (trainings, conferences, books (traditional, e-book, audio books), schooling bills and other type of continuous development expenses);

Negative result: You spend more than you get – in this case you are definitely on your downward spiral; you tend to cover your imbalance by using credit cards or personal loans to make ends meet each month; this adds up each month to increased payments on loans and credit cards and if your income doesn't grow fast you will find yourself soon enough in financial trouble; you have only two options to exit this vicious cycle: cut costs and save some money to make end meet or find solutions and new sources of income to grow your monthly cash inflow!

Positive result: You get more than you spend – some will say it is the perfect case; if you have all your spending covered, your savings and investments in the rate portion, your investments in yourself and your development included and all your needs are filled, you may be one of the lucky ones; you have the chance to increase your investments, either in yourself of your financial future, or you may spend some of the extra money on increasing your life style.

What is your situation?

Maybe your one of the lucky ones and you face a positive result. Good for you and I think you can go to the next chapters to review some of the secrets of personal budgeting or see if you may find some new tips and tricks to increase your financial success.

Maybe you are on neutral result. It is good and you may find useful things on how to optimize the way you manage and use your money on the next step.

Are you in your downward spiral? Do you face negative result on your budget? Do not give-up yet! You are still in the position to change your financial situation. Let's learn together how to balance and then optimize your budget.

Before optimizing the way you manage your money, you have to ensure that you have a positive or a neutral result from your budgeting exercise. If you have a positive result it is a really easy task to balance your budget and get to neutral result. Just decide how you want to invest your extra money. Is it about your financial future by increasing your savings? Is it about your personal development by increasing your investments in yourself? Is it about increasing your lifestyle and life comfort?

What should you do if you are on the negative result situation?

As I stated earlier, you have two options: cutting costs or finding solutions to increase income.

Cutting costs is usually the fastest solution to balance your budget. It is in fact a three step process and it goes like this:

1. Identify how much you have to cut in order to balance the budget and the exact amounts you spend on every type of expense
2. Decide in detail how much you afford cut from each type of expense
3. Do the budgeting exercise and check if your result is as expected.

First step you already did when you started the budgeting exercise. Or at least, I hope you did. At this point you should know how far you are from a neutral result and what you're spending really are.

Money Management

REMEMBER: *The tracking expenses exercise is vital to your financial health to be aware about your real spending on each type of expense. You should do it as soon as possible.*

Ok, let's assume that you did it. Now what? Let's go together to the second step of the balancing process.

Take a deep look on your spending journal and find out what are the areas where you can afford to make the cuts.

Cutting from the small ticket size but regular expenses usually do the trick. Do you really need that coffee-to-go on your way to the office? Do you really need that newspaper that usually lands in the garbage unread? How about cable TV? A cheaper package wouldn't be enough? Are you really watching all those channels?

Cutting costs on the things that are nice to have but you don't really use is a good start. You should consider all the expenses generated by the silly game I mentioned earlier: "Keeping-up with the Jones's". Let's look to your car, clothes and other "status" objects. Are they really what you want or are they the result of that stupid game?

How about your entertainment or recreation spending? Are all of them really necessary? Can you cut something off?

Keep a clear record of all your habitual spending. The spending journal will give you insights you did not been aware about before on where your money actually flies. It will also bring you, ideas to adjust your budget if the real cost is higher on particular aspects. Spending patterns and hidden habits that will rise might surprise you!

REMEMBER: *Make cuts in your expenses wisely! It is vital to remain realistic and keep your living expenses in our focus when you take decisions.*

Another strategy to cut some of your costs is to set up a bill payment plan and to consolidate the payments.

How can you consolidate your payments? You may consider contracting a real-estate property management company and having a single payment for all your housing costs (utilities, reparations, maintenance, etc.). They will charge you a fee but it may be less than the banking fees that you pay when you pay everything yourself.

Consolidating your payments into one single payment can make a significant difference from the costs point of view by reducing banking fees and by budgeting point of view by aligning it with your real inflow of money.

Money Management

What is the amount of your money inflow and when it really happens will influence your budgeting exercise.

If you have your cash inflow monthly at the end of the month, you may consider consolidating and setting a payment plan accordingly.

If you get your money twice a month, at the middle and at the end, you may consider having all big ticket payments from one of the two moments and keeping the other for daily living expenses. Or, you may choose to make baking payments (mortgage, personal loans, credit card, etc.) at one moment and housing and other regular payments at the second.

If you get paid weekly you may plan your payments according to the amounts you get at each payment. The same approach could work if you have multiple sources of income.

Of course, there is and it always will be the threat of rising interest rates, inflation and unexpected events to deal with. Whatever you can do to cut the costs will bring immense benefit you financial health.

Sometimes cutting costs is not enough to make the end of the month and end of your cash meet.

The second way to balance the budget is finding solutions to increase your income.

The fastest and easiest way is to go extra-hours to your current job. This will bring you some extra cash that can make the difference.

How about when this is not possible? You have to find innovative solutions. Let's explore some ideas to start with and to be an inspiration for your personal situation:

- *Earning more from your current employer*: if going extra-hours do not work it does not mean that there are no solution to earn more money from your current employer; as you realized I stated earning more from your current employer and not current job; there are most of the times potential to take more responsibilities and/or different tasks to get you a rise; of course, in some cases you will need to develop your skills or even to learn new ones; this is way continuous investment in yourself is vital for your financial health;

- *Looking for a new job (full-time/part-time)*: sometimes your current job will not bring you the extra-cash you need; it is time to go for a new job; assess your skills, knowledge and expertise and go for it; you may consider even taking a part-time job for start to balance the budget faster;

- *Freelancing*: is a very good way to keep your current job and start earning some cash in your spare-time;

- *Starting a home-based business*: like in the freelancing case it is the cheapest way to start a business; the recent internet developments made it even easier; unfortunately, it increased also the number of scams that claim to make you rich instantly or "while you sleep"; you have to look out of this type of scams to avoid losing your money and increasing your imbalance in your budget.

REMEMBER: ***When balancing your budget finding solutions to get your income to your needs is as important as cost cutting.***

Your current behavior has brought you where you are now. If your financial vision is different from your current situation you should consider changing something. Finding creative and original allocation of your inflow is the key.

Balance and revise your budget regularly. Personal budgeting is a dynamic process. It is the living proof of your financial health. Work on it regularly to keep it fit.

Step 5: Optimize your money management

Balancing your budget, working on it regularly and keeping it fit, is as I already mentioned the sign of your current financial health. Optimizing the way you use and manage your money it what will ensure your future financial health and prosperity.

You should always be focused on the future. What do you want to achieve with your money management process? What is your dream and goal and where you are on your journey to achieve it?

Managing money is not an event. Money management is a process and should become your lifestyle.

As you evolve, your needs, dreams and desires evolve and change. In this case your way to handle and manage your money should be changed regularly to align with your new vision about your future.

In the same time, you may face some unexpected events in life and you may need to make adjustments to your budget. Unexpected loses and even unexpected gains influence your lifestyle, your vision and your budget. Changing budgets should be seen as a process of life and proof that you are in control of your financial health.

Be always prepared to face some of these types of situations:

- *Changes of interest rates*: work on your debt; pay a little extra every month on your debt; may start with the smaller one and when you are done with it move all the payments that you were making to the next one; with these "snowball effect" you will be able to get-out-of-debt in 5-7 years regardless of how much is your debt now;

- *Changes of income*: we live in turbulent times and you may never know for sure how your income will evolve for long term; be prepared by having a buffer fund and regularly investing in your development; put 10% of your regular income in this buffer fund and 10% for your development; you may start smaller at first and increase the percentages until you meet the 10% for each of them;

- *Relocation*: there some events that will make you relocate; the buffer fund it is the answer; work on your buffer fund until it can cover six to nine monthly expenses;

- *Family growing*: this type of event are most of the times joyful moments; in the same times they bring with them some changes in your budget; make your budgeting exercise flexible enough to be able to make the adjustments when needed;

- *Unexpected expenses*: keeping your budgeting flexible it can be a life saver in some situations; you can meet some situations when the buffer fund will not be enough; be prepared to include in your budget a new loan installment if case you need to;

REMEMBER: *Optimizing your management of money is about planning ahead and being prepared to face almost anything that might happen into your life.*

If you understand that money management is a lifestyle and that optimizing the way you manage your money should be a part of your regular activities, if you see this exercise as a means to your goals and dreams, you will be able to benefit from it to the max.

Plan you financials, stick to your budget, get out of debt as fast as you can and stay out of debt, pay your bills and dues at the time, keep a clear record of your spending, and you will be able to have an optimal money management system to meet your dreams even faster that you plan.

Money Management

THE SECRETS OF MONEY MANAGEMENT

There are a lot of people that think about actively managing their money. Some of them even make the budgeting exercise once or twice. A smaller number try it for a while and then decide that is not working for them.

Why is this happening? How come so many people plan to do it and so few succeed in their financial endeavor? What are the secrets that the few people that succeed use?

There are some secrets I have learned from my financially successful clients and you are about to learn them.

Secret #1 Full responsibility

I have met during my 15 years banking career a lot of successful and not so financially successful people.

I remember some of my customers I have met in my early years that started from really poor condition and now own and run million dollars companies. In the same time there are some of the clients that are in the same financial condition like 10 years ago. They struggle every month to cover their expenses and do a lot effort to stay above the water. There are also some clients that are actually in a worse financial condition like 2 or 3 years ago.

What happened? What makes the difference between those people?

When I talk to the ones that are really successful with their financial life, all the time they talk about how they make things happen. They always talk about what they did and how it turned into their life. They know what they invested in their business, in themselves, in their teams. They seem to have a clear view about what made the difference and what lead them to success.

I once heard someone saying that you are "the total of your past actions". You are responsible for who and where you are now and you are the only one who can change it.

This is the most important difference between successful people and unsuccessful ones. They assume responsibility for all their decisions and actions. They know that they are the only ones responsible for the situation that they are facing.

On the other hand, the unsuccessful ones are most of the time blaming economy, government, spouse or partner and anyone else except themselves. They are always ready to give you examples how others are responsible for their situation. And a lot of them are rather good on that. They find so many and logical arguments that you might really believe them.

Think about it for a minute! If someone else is responsible for your situation where it puts you? Who is in control of your life? Are you really free? What can you do? Are you willing to sit and wait for a miracle? Are you waiting for someone else to work for you?

The Bible puts it pretty clear: "Whatever a man sows, that he shall also reap." You have to do something about your situation. Get all your courage and be able to accept that you are the only one responsible for your own well-being. You have to start working the ground and sowing in order to prepare the crops and to be able to reap at the right time.

One comedian said it: "if your father is not a millionaire is not your fault, if your father-in-law is not a millionaire is your entire fault." It is the same with your financial situation. The external conditions, the shape of your economy are not your fault; your own financial health is your entire responsibility.

REMEMBER: *YOU are the only one responsible to change your life and your financial situation!*

Secret #2 Managing decision

Tony Robbins says that in order to succeed you have to take "massive action". In the same time you may have heard the "Success is a decision away!"

A lot of motivational speakers and self-help gurus talk about the power of decision and the importance of acting upon that decision.

If you got the 1st secret, you know that it is pretty obvious that it is your responsibility to decide what you want and to act towards your goal.

You maybe know someone who decided to start managing his/her money and even took action and did it for a while. And at some point they stopped doing it and said that is not working for their situation. Even came with pretty logical arguments about how their external conditions changed so dramatically that it is not working anymore.

Here comes the second secret. You have to manage your decisions over time.

Think about people that start dieting to lose some weight. You notice that they usually succeed for a while and, after a short period you see them gaining all the weight back. What happened? They made the decision. They took action. They even saw some results. They weren't able to manage their decision over time. Their motivation faded away or they saw the results and went back to the old habits.

It is the same with money management. Remember that managing your money is a process that you have to do on the daily basis.

When talking to the most successful clients I realized that they always knew their financial situation. Even the ones with multi-million businesses were aware about their personal financial health. They always knew and were able to tell if something is in their budget or not. And the surprise was that if they decided that is not or they cannot afford it at that moment they postpone the buying.

The fact that you need a financial plan or a personal budget to succeed in your financial area is not a secret and most of the people know it. As you already saw on the first secret you have to work it out. The big problem is that most of the people that understand the first secret are not able to master the second secret. They plan and instead of working the plan they dig a hole of debt by going and making expenses that are not in the budget. And they always have a good reason for that purchase.

REMEMBER: *Manage your decisions over time and always focus on your desired goal; is this particular decision getting you closer to your financial goal or it is only and short-term superficial*

pleasure that will keep you away to
reaching your dream?

You have to start managing your decision over time. Start small. Take the decision to track you spending. Do it daily for a month or two. Get a grasp of it and increase the decision to the next level. Balance your budget. Exercise for a while. Keep increasing the decision and grow your money management skills.

Secret #3 Dealing with setbacks

One surprising thing I have learned from my financially successful customers was that they lost some money on the way to their success. And most of them were telling me that with no regret or guilt or shame. They were more focused on the lesson they learned from that experience than from losing the money itself.

As in any new beginning, when you begin your journey to financial health, you encounter some setbacks. You may face some challenges regarding sticking to the financial plan. You may feel very hard to keep track to every single spending. You may find challenging to keep your budget balanced every single month. There are a lot of possible setbacks. And if you find yourself in front of a setback don't make it a bigger deal that it really is.

Remember when you learned to walk. Or just watch little kids how they learn to walk. They try to get up; they fall and try again until they make it. They don't give up after first, second or third fall they take. They keep pushing until they make it.

Do the same when it comes to money management. You are a little kid that is learning to walk the road to financial success and money management is your first step. Give yourself permission to make some mistakes at first.

There is a saying about what happens when a rich and inexperienced man meets an experienced one. Both end up having what they need: the inexperienced with experience and the experienced with the money. Allow yourself to make some mistakes and learn from each of them the lesson it teaches you.

Is it realistic? Can you really keep a positive attitude when you deal with setbacks? Use what little kids use. They are encouraged by the parents even when they fell. Partner with some when you start actively managing your money. You may use a professional counselor or just use your family support. Use the power of encouragement and get use to celebrate the small successes.

REMEMBER: *Set-backs are only lessons that life teaches us; take the lesson and leave the setback behind you; you are on your way to your dream; keep going forward.*

Secret #4 Compound interest

Albert Einstein allegedly said that compound interest is the most powerful force he has ever seen. How come the man how revolutionized physics and understood the power of atomic forces can states that compound interest is the most powerful force?

What exactly is compound interest? Basically compound interest is interest that is collected on the original amount and is added up to the total to generate interest. So in simple term is interest that generates interest. To be more close to reality in actually money that grows from itself. This means that compound interest is the closest thing to "perpetual mobile" concept.

For example, if you put 100$ every month from your child is born until he gets 18 in a piggy bank, you will save 1200$ every year. When he/she will turn 18 you'll be able to give a nice 21.600$ birthday gift.

If you do the same thing but you put that 100$ in a savings account every month and you do it only until he/she get to 10 years old. If you get an average interest rate for the 18 years of only 5% per year, when he/she will turn 18 you'll be able to give just a little more than 24.000$ birthday gift, and all this only with the effort of 100$ a month for 10 years, meaning 12.000$.

If you put the same amount for the same time, but you use a typical investment fund with an average return of 8% per year, and you forget about it, when he/she will turn 65 and hit the retirement age, he/she will have over 1.2 million dollars in the account! Imagine, over 1.2 million from initial 12.000$ invested in 10 years! This is the power of compound interest!

The secret of compound interest is to use it properly. Unfortunately, for most people compound interest is working against them. If you neglect to pay your loans and credits they will build up faster that you can imagine.

Let's see how you can use it even when it is on your loans. For example if you have a 100,000$ mortgage for 20 years and your interest rate is 7% per year. If you choose to make an extra payment of only 65$ every month you'll save about 15.000$ from interest paid and you will shorten the period with 3 years. Doing the same thing but with 100$ extra payment each month you will save close to 21.000$ and over 4 years on the payment period. And all this is reached for less than 4$ per day.

REMEMBER: *Compound interest*
can work for you or against you.
Use the power of compound
interest in your favor and
nothing will stop you on your
financial success journey.

Pay your debts as fast as you can and start saving from day one of your active and conscious money management endeavor.

Start with a small amount of extra payments for your loans and even smaller amounts for your savings if necessary but keep doing it and you'll reap the rewards of financial discipline.

Secret #5 Multiple sources of income

One other secret I have learned from my financial successful clients is actually not a real secret. It is something that we all know or, at least, we think about from time to time.

The financial successful people have always applied this secret. They always developed multiple sources of income as early as possible in their journey to financial success. If one of the income streams fail due to external factors (economic downturn, mismanagement, etc.), they have a back-up income stream to rely.

The situation that we are now living in - inflation, economic developments and all the social and political factors - requires you to have more incomes to keep you on the safe side. Everybody should develop multiple sources of income to rely on in this insecure economic environment.

How can you create more than one source of income in your life? If you are like the most people you are now relying on your current job income. Here are some ideas to find some extra income sources:

-    Real-estate investing: think about investing in real-estate and renting the property; the current market is the perfect place to invest in real-estate; as Baron Rothschild said in 19th century: *"Buy when there's blood in the streets"*; maybe you cannot see the blood on the street but there is blood on bank accounts;

- Dividends: go ahead and start investing in stocks, bonds, or investment funds; if you do not have a big amount to block in a real-estate investment you may start smaller by using investing in some funds or buying stocks and bonds; using the investment funds is more comfortable due to the fact the management of your investment is done by some professionals and in the same time you may start with smaller amounts;

- Get a part-time job: you may consider to get a part-time engagement with some marketing company and get involved in projects (mystery shopping, surveys, paid focus groups, etc.) or offer basic services (babysitting, dog walking, house cleaning, gardening, etc.);

- Freelance: if you have some special skills you may consider freelancing and selling your skill yourself; specialized services like tutoring, consulting, design (home interior, garden, logo, etc.), and any other type of services may turn into an extra income stream.

Most people unfortunately rely only on one source of

income and when they lose it due to some unexpected events they face a really big problem. The loss not only has a terrible impact on their financial life but it may affect their emotional and physical well-being.

REMEMBER: *Imagine your financial life as a table: if you have a one legged table it has all the chances to fall if the leg is not centered and thick enough; the more legs you have, the more stable your table will be and the less thicker legs will need.*

Developing more than one source of income offers a safety net from both financial and psychological point of view.

Secret #6 Passive vs. active income

All the financial successful people know about what Robert Kiyosaki presents in Cash Flow Quadrant. Maybe they don't know it in the same words as Mr. Kiyosaki states it, but they are aware about different types of income and how they can use them. There are two main types of incomes: active income and passive income.

Money Management

How many times are you paid for what you do now?

Most of the people are paid only once. Regardless if the create something in a factory, the do a report in an office, they sell something to a customer, most of the people are paid only for the result of the specific action. The active income is the type of income that you get only when you do some work. It is the type of money that you earn for putting your time, effort and skill into action. The active income is present only when you actively do something. The active income means you working for your money.

On the other hand, the passive income is when you are paid over and over again for an action you took once. You may have heard about it as residual income. If you look again on the secret#5 you'll notice that the first 2 examples are about passive income. They generate on going income for an action that you took once. One time investment in a real-estate property or some stock will generate future incomes as rent or dividends for years and years to come.

Passive income is what you may call making money while you sleep or putting money to work for you.

One type of passive income is the one that a lot of people have without realizing the importance of it. It is about interest.

Remember the compound interest? Interest you gain from you savings is a passive income source. You already have a passive income source in your life. Just go now and diversify your passive income sources.

Take your time and get an honest assessment about your situation. How much of your income is from active income streams and how much of it is from passive income stream? How about changing this ratio? Think about how you can develop some passive income streams. Can you invest in real-estate or investment funds? What are your hobbies? Can you start making money from your hobbies like getting royalties for your pictures and videos? How about your networking skills? You may consider joining a MLM or network marketing business.

Changing the ratio between your active and passive income streams is the key of optimal money management. It is the moment when you really find the best use for your money. You put the money to work for you instead permanently working yourself to get the money.

REMEMBER: ***Putting your money to work for you is the best use you can find for them. This is the essence on money management!***

Secret #7 Keep it simple

Most of the people, when think about money management, they tend to develop a lot of complex systems to keep track of their money. They start studying and learning complex financial concepts about loans, credits score calculation and investments. They are very eager to put in practice all that concepts and ideas. At the end they finish by developing a huge system that is very hard to work with.

In fact the reality is a little bit different. Having in mind that over 90% of the people are employed and most of their inflow of money comes from only one place, their salary, tracking and recording your spending and your spending habits for a month will provide you a very good image about your finances and your financial path. How do you spend in the first few days after your salary gets into your account? Do you keep the same spending habits for the entire month or you tend to make impulse purchases mainly just after your paycheck? Do you have most of your regular payments gathered in the first days after your salary day or are they scattered during all month?

On the other hand, it is rather difficult to record all of your spending for that long. You may feel that you really need those complex ideas and solutions to make your life easier.

In fact, we live in a complex world and it is somewhat understandable. For instance, I have to recognize that I do not have a clue how more than half of the tools I use every day are working. And from the rest, for most of them have only a vague idea about how they actually work. I use the computer in front of me to type the manuscript of this book and I have to tell you that I am totally unaware about what it makes it work. I have an idea about bits and bytes and ones and zeros but that is pretty much it. It is the same with all the house appliances. All this lack of knowledge does not keep me from using them. It is the same case with money management. Keep it simple!

Here are a few ideas about keeping the money management as simple as possible:

- Money management tool #1: A simple notebook; always keep a simple plain page notebook with your wallet; every time you take your wallet out to make a payment you will have to take out the notebook too;

- Money management tool #2: A blue ink pen; you have to be prepared to record every payment that you are making in the moment you are making it; yes, you get a receipt for your transaction but most of the receipts get lost and taking 15 minutes every evening to record your daily transaction can be perceived like an unnecessary burden at some moments; at the same time, you will be able to write any idea or thought about solutions regarding managing your money that comes through you mind and review it later on when you have time;

- Money management action #1: analyze regularly your spending habits and choose one type of habit you want to work on; is it about impulse driven purchases? Decide to postpone every purchase to be able to figure out if it is really needed of a moment's impulse. Is it about spending too much before regular payments (loan installments, housing, etc.)? Find solutions to get all of them in the first days after your salary of make some special accounts to keep the money until you pay the bills.

The most important part when building your money management system is keeping a very good record of how you spend every single cent. During my extensive banking career I had the chance to meet a lot of financially successful people. Very few of them were able to build their fortune by managing their money without this kind of specific money tracking. The fact is that all the financial unsuccessful people I have encountered in the same time did not keep this type of records.

REMEMBER: *Keep it simple and easy to use!*

TIPS AND TRICKS OF MONEY MANAGEMENT

When I talk to every financial successful person that I meet I am totally surprised to see that every single one tells me the same 3 main things:

- Pay your debt;

- Start saving and investing;

- Grow your income.

Here you will explore some of the most practical methods to help you all three areas.

Dealing with debt

One shocking surprise I had when I asked my wealth clients about how they deal with personal debt the answer was: "What personal debt?"

One of the first things the riches do is not to have debt in their financial life. There are a lot of myths about debt and debt management. Let's explore some of them and then figure out how you can improve your money management on dealing with debt.

Understanding debt

There are some financial experts and money management gurus that are promoting "good debt" versus "bad debt". Maybe you are one of the people that think this too. Let's explore some truths about debt.

What is debt? If you check the Collins's World English Dictionary, you will find some definitions like "something that is owed, such as money, goods, or services", "an obligation to pay or perform something, a liability", or even better "a temporary failure to maintain the necessary supply of something: sleep debt; oxygen debt". In your case, you can say it is about "failure to maintain the necessary supply of money".

So how come there can be something like "good debt"? What those so-called financial experts say? Most of them define "good debt" like something that you do not afford or do not have the resources to pay for up front, but have the potential to pay on a schedule, such as big ticket size acquisitions: houses and/or cars.

Ok, it can be a good explanation. Unfortunately the most people misunderstand this explanation and translate into their mind like: something you do not afford or do not have the resources to pay for up front and **you are allowed** to pay on a schedule. They base their decision by the fact that they are allowed to pay on a schedule and not on having the potential of possibilities to make those payments fit into their present and future financial budget.

On the other hand, most people tend to forget that any kind of debt comes with an interest. You already saw the power of compound interest.

How can you use the power of interest for you when you are in debt? As you already saw is making the extra-payments.

5 Step Debt Solution

As we agreed that there is no such thing as "good debt" or at least not for you, but for the bank, the only way to deal with debt is to find solutions to get out of it.

Here is a simple and powerful 5 step solution how to manage to get debt-free faster.

Manage your money

A getting out of debt solution cannot work without managing your money actively and consciously. I am aware about how much pressure I am putting on keeping a record about your spending and spending habits, but you have to believe me that your chances of getting out of debt without being aware about your spending habits it is close to zero. Your spending habits brought you here. You have to change some of them if you really plan to change your financial life.

Money Management

You have to make a budget and find the right solutions to balance it. Whether is about cost cutting or about increasing incomes, you have to find the optimal solutions for your own situation.

Make the list

The second step is about making an objective and comprehensive assessment of your debts. List all your debts, the exact amount for each of them, the interest rates, and the minimum payments. You can structure the list from the interest rate point of view, or minimum payment point of view.

Some of the financial experts recommend you to pay the higher interest rate debts first. There is logic behind it. If you pay the higher interest rate debts, you save on interest rate paid. In the same time, if the high interest rate debts have high minimum payments, how much will count an extra payment of 50$ a month? As you already saw in the compound interest exercise, for the mortgage payment is less than 3 years.

Start paying the lowest minimum payment debt first. It will make every cent of your extra payments count. In the same time, after this loan is gone and you will be able to move entire monthly payments and the extra payments that you are already used to against the next one. You will start to see the effects of snow ball you started.

Money Management

Some financial experts will tell you about making a calculus about how much money you pay or save on the long run if you choose one of the two approaches. Sometimes they will bring in the "big guns" like net-present-value of your money and future-value and return-on-investment concepts into the game.

REMEMBER: *You as me and as any financial successful people are only a human. You need motivation on the long run and seeing and feeling results is better than complex financial concepts. Keep it simple and easy to use!*

Manage your decision

Ok, you already know how do you stand and how you will proceed. It is time to take action and keep on going. This third step is the one that make all the difference between your successes of your unsuccessful endeavors.

A lot of people take very seriously the first two steps; they even go further and make a deep calculus about what they will pay and how much they will get from every single cent of extra payment made of each of the current debts. They start the process and at some point they feel it becoming so hard to manage and the pressure increasing so rapidly so they throw the towel. They just give up and conclude that is not for them. In other cases, it is about an unexpected event that comes along the way and turns their budget upside down.

When you start thinking about getting out of debt, you have to have three aspects into your focus.

Debt extra payments

It is essential to have an amount of extra payment that really makes a difference. Yes, every single cent counts and helps you make interest work for you and not against you.

On the other hand not every cent is made equal. The extra payments made on the smallest amounts will keep you focused on how your debt is going down faster and you will be able to shift the minimum payment and the extra payments to the next debt in a shorter time to see how the effect is growing like a snow ball.

Saving and investing

It could sound paradoxical that you must save in the same time when you are focusing to get out of debt; the common sense will tell you to focus on routing all your income to extra payments to get out of debt faster.

This is the biggest difference between the most financial successful people thinking pattern and the financial unsuccessful common sense driven behaviors. You have to starch a little bit and start saving and investing in the same time. You may face unexpected event along your journey out of debt and you should be prepared to handle them in the best way possible.

On the other hand, I am stressing again that money management is not only about keeping track of where your money goes and living within your means, but more important about finding solutions and opportunities to increase your income to the levels you want. How would you be able to notice and/or act upon the opportunities if you have no cash in hand?

Personal money

One of the biggest mistakes that most of the people make is about cutting all their personal money from the budget when they start to think about getting out of debt.

Hey, you are just a human! You need recreation, you need fun, and you need challenge and development. You have to have some personal money in your budget unless you are on really awful financial situation and really close to bankruptcy.

Paying debt will not have to make you a martyr and it should not be a punishment for I do not know what sins you may think you have like spending recklessly until now.

Optimize along the way

Getting out of debt is a medium term process. Depending on your particular financial situation it could take somewhere to 7 years. In this time you have to optimize your journey regularly.

Money Management

Be always aware of what is happening on your financial situation and how it affects you. How the interest rates are changing? How do these changes influence your minimum payments and the effect of extra payments that you make?

You choose to do it on paper in order to keep in simple or you may use some computer help if you face more than one influence/change in the same time. There are a lot of free resources over the internet that helps you calculate the effect of the extra payments, the effects of interest rate changes and much more.

It is rather simple to choose one of these tools and start using it. I prefer the free ones offered by Bankrate.com. It is simple to use and gives pretty clear images about the effect of interest rate and extra payments. You just enter the debt information, the extra payments you plan and you can get a pretty good image about how your financial situation will evolve.

Celebrate success

Getting out of debt may feel like the biggest duty in your life, particularly if you have a big amount on your balance. Of course it takes some effort and some discipline, but if you can deal with your minimum payments now and you stretch a bit for the extra monthly payments, you will see the results.

Make a habit on celebrating every success. Every debt that you finish with, even the smallest amount ones, are a victory on your debt-free-life journey. Use your personal money and celebrate to keep your motivation up all the way.

Saving and Investing

Money management is a process and a lifestyle. Its main focus should be to help you face all the expected and unexpected events properly and to prepare you to seize all the opportunities that will appear.

In order to do that, you may need to find some ways to start saving and investing your money wisely. There are two aspects to consider:

- reducing your expenses and making room for your saving and investing options;
- saving and investing itself.

Here are some ideas to explore when you are thinking about these two areas of money management.

Reducing expenses

Reducing expenses, or in other words cost cutting, is not the funniest and pleasurable thing to think about. At a first glance, you may consider that you are disciplined enough regarding your spending and there is no room for reducing your expenses.

You may be right. Just take a brief look on the next ideas and see if there is one or even more that you can apply in your life:

Spend only the money you have

Most common mistake people make is to spend their future money. They plan and budget salary increases, bonuses, and even inheritances that never come to reality and they get themselves into financial trouble. Money management is about managing what you have to create what you desire.

REMEMBER: *Manage only what you have and stop managing what you hope and dream about.*

Stick to your budget

Make your budget realistic and based on your needs and never accept to go over the budget. One place where most of the people overspend and go over the budget is groceries and daily habits. It may seem very small mounts but they may break down your discipline. You may have to develop distaste for Starbucks and learn to stick to your grocery list. One simple and yet powerful idea is never go shopping when hungry.

Balance your budget regularly

Keep track of your spending the daily basis. Either you use a notebook or you just keep the receipts at the end of each day, take an overview of your expenditures. You will start very soon to notice some patterns. At the end of each week or month, depending on how your income flows in, groups the daily lists and check where you tend to overspend. In the same time, you should look whether you invest enough. Do you invest in your development? Do you save and invest your money on a regular basis? Keep a constant focus on your financial situation. This, not only gives you a clear image about your current situation, but also might be helpful in controlling your habit to spend, and may motivate you to go further on your way to the financial future you desire.

Stop impulse driven purchases

Keeping a clear record about your spending will help you identify the type of impulse driven purchases you are used to make. Before even thinking to pay for something, ask yourself: Do I really need this? Think on various solutions how you can do without that particular thing. When it comes to high ticket items go and sleep on your decision. Give yourself a good night sleep to find solutions to manage your life without that specific item. If you rationally cannot find other solution, it may be that it is really a need and you probably have to make that purchase. In this case start an extensive research before deciding to buy from a specific location. Consider not only the price, but the durability and quality, the post-sale service and maintenance costs, and all the related aspects. Buying everything on the smallest price could have a big impact on long-term expenses.

Focus on you financial goals

Keep your mind and your attention on your financial goals all the time. When you go shopping, remind yourself what your objective is and ask yourself: is this particular acquisition moving me forward, or is it keeping me from reaching my goals? You might realize that you do not need that 500$ shoes when you can find something similar with 200$. You might realize that you do not need the latest electronic gadget if it will increase the time to meet your goal by six months or even a year.

Use cash

It is very powerful way to stop the small ticket impulse purchases. When you pay with your card you may not be aware all the time about your balance and you may find yourself over the budget without even noticing it. Get your money out of your account and start paying everything in cash! When you notice that the amount of bills is decreasing, you will tend to stop the spending rate. It is a very good way to keep track of your balance. When you feel your pockets empty, you are at your budget's limit.

Stop wasting

We tend to overspend hundreds of dollars on stuff that we don't use. Learn to use every little thing you purchase. Reuse leftovers from the last night's dinner and switch off lights and appliances. Pack your lunch and develop distaste for to-go coffee. It may seem a little bit extreme, but it will save you hundreds, or even thousands of dollars each year. After you start keeping track on your expenses you will notice that about 10%, or in some cases, close to 20% of your total expenses can be saved by these types of simple actions.

Eat wise and healthy

Stop throwing your money on those doughnuts and junk-food. Yes, from time to time, it is a real pleasure to indulge yourself in some of this kind of action. Remember that you are the one responsible for your well-being not only financially, but in all aspects of your life. You can perform at your best when your health and energy level are at their peak. For the day to day meals think about nutritious, food sources instead junk-food. It may feel a little expensive at the first glance but you may find out that you can find nutritious and healthy food on affordable prices too. Think about grains, lentils, legumes and beans. Turn yourself towards water. Plain old water Is cheap and it can replace all high sugar beverages.

Become a free resource fan

We are living in an incredible environment. Internet is providing so many opportunities and so many freebies. Start using the open source and free software. Get your e-book instead of on paper ones and save from that. Training programs and free newsletter may provide you so much information.

In the same time think about other free opportunities you have. Go and exercise outdoors and use your body weight instead of all those machineries in the gym. Give up to your expensive gym membership and enjoy the nature.

Keep your credit cards out of rich

You may consider even cutting your credit card off. Yes, I know it is comfortable to know that you have an extra source of money as on the credit card. In this case, stash the credit card somewhere safe and do not touch it anymore. As the old saying is going: "out of sight, out of mind". Stop caring the credit card with you. It is very hard to resist temptation. You may even consider giving-up to internet banking option. At least for a while until you get disciplined enough. Or, you may choose to have a separate account with a very clear limit for internet purchases. It will help you with managing your money better. In the same time, it will keep your main account safe from any internet related fraud.

Pay yourself first

Develop a habit to pay yourself. Stretch your budget and take off 10% from day one when your income arrives in your account. In this way you will be forced to keep your expenses under control and you will start saving.

REMEMBER: *If you manage to get a positive result on you budgeting exercise, save, invest, or pay your debt. You have no legal requirement to spend everything you earn!*

Saving and investing solutions

As much as important saving and investing is, there are many methods to start this process. All the financial successful people are considering not only one method but they develop saving and investing portfolios. Choosing the best method or methods is determined by your personal situation and your own future financial goals.

Yourself

You are the most important part of your financial picture. You should start and keep investing in yourself. Even in the most troubling situation keep the level of investing in your own development at least at 10% from your income.

In some cases, 10% of your income could be pretty small. Open a savings account and deposit 10% of your income for investing in yourself[1]: trainings, conferences, books, audio and video products.

---

[1] These 10% of your income are different from the 10% mentioned when I was talking about paying yourself first.

Money Management

Remember that you are the most important asset that you have. Your personal and professional development is the base of your success in all areas of life. You are the only one responsible about all your outcomes. Keep this 10% rather fix in any conditions. If needed cut other expenses. You may even choose not to pay yourself first in full and keep the investment in your growth at 10%.

Checking accounts with interest

This is not actually a saving option due to the fact that you have total access to your funds. You benefit from all the checking account accessibilities, while your cash in making money for you through the interest rate. Of course, there is a minimum amount that should be on your balance daily. It may be different from bank to the bank and the usual amount about 2000$. If you consider this minimum amount as your emergency fund you may opt having this type of saving tool in your portfolio.

Savings accounts

These are the perfect way to start saving. When just started the saving process you may even consider requesting an automated payment from your checking account to your saving account in the day one of your income in order to pay yourself first.

Saving accounts are also perfect for short and long-term saving goals and in the same time they can act as emergency funds when needed. The easy access to the money it is both an advantage when thinking about unexpected events or a disadvantage when thinking on the opportunity to cover the budget deficit.

"CD" or Certificates of Deposit

This type of saving is a medium term saving opportunity. It basically and in simple terms "lending" your fund to the state or a financial institution for a certain period, usually from one month to five even seven years. Do an extensive research before choosing in which type of CD's to invest. There are many variables to consider. In some cases, the insurance companies offer better interest rates compared to banks but in the same time the risk may be higher. There are CD's with limited interest withdrawal or that can pay the interest only at the maturity. You should consider professional counseling before investing in CD's.

Money market insured accounts

This type of saving is perfect for you long-term goals. It generally offers a higher interest rate compared to regular saving accounts and the fact that is insured on the money market gives relative independence from your banks interest policies. The interest rate is highly dependent on the amount you have on your balance.

Investment funds

Investment funds are definitely long term investments. They are dedicated to people that really understand the power of compound interest. Why is that? Basically investment funds are a set of stock, bond, money market securities and other financial instruments bundled in the way to optimize the return and minimize the risk. Does it mean that they are risk free? Not at all. It means only that for a specifically expected return, you will face the minimum risk possible at that right moment. Over time, the usual return from a medium risk investment fund may vary from 5% to 9% while returns over this limit carry a higher risk. For example, the stock market may give you returns over 10%, but in the same time there are a lot of the stocks that go down even on an increasing market.

The value of your investment is provided daily by NAV (net asset value) that is calculated on overall holdings of the fund by adding all the assets and subtracting all the liabilities.

There is another aspect when thinking about investment funds besides return and the risk they carry. It is about heir liquidity, meaning how fast you have access to your money at the minimal fees and discount price.

One other important thing you should check about an investment fund is its Prospectus. It is the legal document that states all about the type of holdings that the fund is comprised of, the risks and the expected returns, the fees and liquidity, the insurance if there is any, and other important legal aspects.

The biggest advantage with the investment funds is that you have a team of professionals managing your investments and you should look only on the investment funds NAV to see how your investment is going. On the other hand, you have no control over your funds more than the ones stated in the Prospectus.

Money Management

Before using this type of investments you should check how the terms stated in the fund's prospectus fits to your needs and goals.

401(K) and other retirement plans

Retirement plans are usually very easy way to start saving for long-term. There may be 401(K) or other type of retirement plans offered by different financial institutions.

Basically they allow you to invest on a regular basis small amount form your income into their investment fund and, when the time of your retirement comes, they provide you the option to have a monthly income or a one-time payment of you total fund.

They are only one other way to invest in investment fund but they provide you some constraints related to your saving habits by their regular deposit requirement.

Stock and bonds

One other type of investment is directly into stocks, bonds and other money and capital market instruments. In this case you have more or less total freedom of decision where, when, and how much to invest. In the same time, it requires a lot of knowledge and research if you want to have in informed decision. Think about this type of solution only after you have enough knowledge and you want to diversify your saving and investing portfolio.

Money Management

Real estate

Investing in real estate is a complex business. It is not only the amounts you need to put in abut also about all the many factors that affect the return on your money. If your financial goal is really on long term, real estate investing could be the perfect fit due to its longer term liquidity.

Having the present situation, probably it is the wisest thing to invest in real estate. As baron Rothschild allegedly mentioned in 19th century: *"Buy when there's blood in the streets"*, meaning buy when the economic situation is down.

The profitability of your real estate investment has five main factors. Besides the real estate market evolution and renting market evolution there are three that are probably the most important ones: location, location, and location. Choosing the right location could be most of the times more important than the market evolution. For example, real-estate prices did grow since 2008 until now in Vienna, Paris, London and other places regardless of economic turmoil that the entire world is facing.

REMEMBER: *Start small and let your money work for you. Develop a portfolio to multiply your sources of income.*

If your financial goals are on the long term, it is a wiser to start saving money as early as possible and let the compound interest to work for you. In time, you can develop a real portfolio of saving and investment instruments that will drive you to financial success. Choosing the right financial partner such as bank, insurance company and brokerage firm may make a lot of difference in time and effort you will have to put in your journey.

Boosting income

As I already mentioned, and I cannot stress it enough, money management is not keeping you in your means, or at least, not only about that. It is focusing your attention to the opportunities to increase your income and to create the financial future you want.

Here you are some ideas to start your creative juices boil up and develop your own income boosting solutions.

Income idea #1 Your hidden talent

What would you do if you find yourself having to support your younger brother and sister when you are still a kid?

The man I'm talking about started with numerous seemingly unimportant jobs. Starting with the age of ten, he went from farmer's help to railroad fireman and sale insurance sales man. At his 40' he was running a service station where he was offering also food. After some time he opened and restaurant across the street from the service station.

Money Management

At the age of 62, after retiring and getting his first retirement check, he decided that he has to find a way to increase his income. In that moment he decided to use the only talent he had: an old recipe of fried chicken. He started going across entire US and trying to convince restaurant owners to use his recipe and pay him a nickel for every chicken sold.

The urban legend says that it took him 2 years to sign the first contract. The fact is that in 12 years, in 1964, there were over 600 franchises across the country. Probably at this moment you already know that I'm talking about Col. Saunders.

If you are like the most people, you definitely have at least one talent. Either you are aware of it or not you should figure it out. Identify your hidden talent and plan how you can monetize it.

You may start by asking yourself what you enjoy doing. Do you enjoy gardening? Do you love to painting or drawing? Are you very good at crosswords? Find out what really makes you tick and develop a plan to make money from it.

You may think on starting a home business on offering gardening services on our free time. You may think selling your goods, if you are in creating things. You may start a partnership with a magazine or a newspaper on providing them crossword puzzles. Or even start your own blog and share your expertise in any area you have.

You can start small, as a part time job and develop a second source of income from your hidden talent.

Income idea #2 Internet income

The amazing development of the internet provides us with countless opportunities. Basically there are two types of ways to make money online: selling products and providing information.

You may consider creating your own online store. You may start by promoting other's products and, by the tie, develop your own real store. It will need some attention to orders, delivery, accounting and all the details related to a store.

On the other way, you may choose to provide information. Creating a blog and sharing your own expertise is a great way to start. Getting followers and recommending products and services may be a very good way to monetize your expertise.

Beware that in both cases that it requires some investment of time and money. The aggressive development of the internet has also its downturn. Building a website with best products at the best prices or with the most accurate information delivered in the most suitable way will not guarantee that you will get the money. You have to put constant effort on updating your website, marketing it to the right targeted customers, and doing all the work needed to make yourself known to the market. If you are not constantly doing it, the chance to have someone on your website by accident is less than winning the lottery.

Income idea #3 Home based business ideas

When asked, a lot of people will say that they would love to have an extra source of income. On the other hand, very few of them even bother to think about what they can do to make it come true. They tend to come with excuses like "I don't have the time" while they are spending the evening on the couch in front of the TV, or "I don't have the money to start a business" while they spend carelessly every day.

I know a man that was a school drop-out. His father was a well-know barrister. Yet, he struggled his way through school until he turned 16 when he decided that this formal education endeavor should end. He dropped-out school and started a very small magazine called "The student". The magazine was promoting music through the student population in London. After some years he started to records promoted in the magazine by a mail-order system. In a couple of years, in 1972, he opened his first record store called Virgin Records. The rest is history. Sir Richard Branson has investments of billions of dollars and all started with a small magazine and selling music records to students. As you can see, even a small idea may lead you in time to great achievements.

Starting and running a home based business provides you a few benefits that other small business does not have. You have your business space for free. You do not have to show up at a set time that your customers know it's open. You can use the skills you

Money Management

already have. You can spend the no-activity moments with your family and if needed you are ready for business in no time.

What can you do as a home based business?

Here are some ideas to consider. Some of them may seem very basic and simple, but remember that simple things are often overlooked.

Network marketing – it one of the most used home based business ideas. Promoting somebody else's products can bring you money with no additional costs with logistics, shipping and handling, not even accounting. Does this really work? As far as there are companies more than 50 years old on this type of business and people involved even from the start and still doing it, should be very good proof that it works. The main issue is choosing the right company for you. Choose one that has a proven track record of business and has the products that you can use and promote. You may think about online network marketing. The rate of scams is very high and the choosing process should take more research;

Running errands – there are a lot of people how would like to outsource the daily chores. Providing this type of services could be a start even for a teenager;

Babysitting, cutting lawn and removing snow – are basic services that you can start providing and getting some extra cash;

Tailoring – if your skills are right you may think not only designing and making your own outfits for fun but making also some money from it; you may start by offering altering services and increase along with your skills;

Outcall beauty services — Make-up, haircut and hairdressing, and other type of beauty services can be performed at home or in the office; in nowadays there are a lot of busy people that may be interested in this type of approach regarding their looks.

Freelance designing services – if you enjoy gardening, you may develop your skills on designing the perfect garden

Event planning – monetize on your organizational and project management skills and provide event planning services.

Marketing research and mystery shopping – there are a lot of marketing agencies in need for partners in marketing surveys and studies.

Tutoring – use your knowledge to help others; you may think on offering tutoring services

Business consulting and/or coaching – use your professional expertise to help other to develop and grow their businesses.

Building furniture — if you have the skills and you enjoy carpeting you may create handmade furniture; selling your products is only about how you market it.

These are only a few ideas to look into in order to train your mind and your thinking pattern towards finding income boosting solutions. I sampled just these ones because are the ones that require the less investment money wise and you can monetize what you already know and have. Most probably none of them will turn into instant million dollar business and some of them not even on the long run. Use them to start focusing your attention from what you don't have and what your limitations are to what you may use and to act on opportunities that may appear.

There are a lot of claims and so-called money experts that will try to sell you "instant-millionaire" and "get-rich-quick" schemes. I am not saying that there are all of them scams but you should be very careful. Usually if it sounds too good to be true most probably is.

REMEMBER: *There is no such thing like a free lunch. You have to do some effort in order to increase your income.*

Money Management

FINAL THOUGHTS ON MONEY MANAGEMENT

Here we are very close to our journey's end and at the start of your own journey to financial success.

Before you start applying all the ideas you found in this book in your daily routine, let me provide you the 4 truths of money management. It is not personal vanity to call the following concepts truths. I use this term to stress the importance of understanding them on the right way and applying all of them in order to ensure your success.

> "As to methods there may be a million and then some, but principles are few. The man who grasps principles can successfully select his own methods. The man, who tries methods, ignoring principles, is sure to have trouble."
>
> Ralph Waldo Emerson

Money Management

Understanding the following truths about money management will make the difference about how successful you will become on your financial life.

1. You are the only one responsible for your outcomes

"I am the master of my fate. I am the captain of my soul."

William Henley (1849-1903)

This is not only a key truth in money management, but it is the main truth of life in general. No one else will make you successful in any area of life. It is all about to you. You are the "master of your fate" and you are fully responsible for your own success.

"Be not angry that you cannot make others as you wish them to be, since you cannot make yourself as you wish to be."

Thomas Kempis (1380-1471)

You have to make a specific and focused effort to be what we really want to be. You must do your duties, complete your tasks, and create the life you desire. There are always temptations for immediate pleasure and here is the moment when money management comes to assist. It is only the tool to support you on your journey.

Money Management

You are unique and you should act on what you believe in, taking responsibility for your actions and outcomes. Money management provides you a good objective look at yourself and it comes in handy in determining what and when your needs change.

"He that is good at making excuses is seldom good for anything else."

Benjamin Franklin (1706-1790)

2. Money management is about growth

"I used to say, 'things cost too much.' Then my teacher straightened me out on that by saying, 'The problem isn't that things cost too much. The problem is that you can't afford it.' That's when I finally understood that the problem wasn't it—the problem was me!"

Jim Rohn (1930 – 2009)

Money management is not about what you cannot afford. It is not about where to stop spending. It is not about a way to limit you.

All the money management is about is finding solutions to keep your spending within your means. And if your means are not big enough for your needs, it helps you grow.

Money Management

Creating a budget and sticking to it, these are only the first steps of money management, and yet these are things that often separate the financially successful people from everyone else. What's next? Now that you have listed your incomes and expenses, identify ways and solutions to increase your earnings, or reduce your spending. Usually you will find ways to do both.

"Invest in yourself. Your career is the engine of your wealth."

Paul Hugh Clitheroe (1955 -)

We all want financial success, but how do we achieve it?

It starts right from you are now. It starts with the first step of defining your dream and making a plan to achieve it. Most of the times, it means changing and improving yourself. It means developing new skills, acquiring new knowledge, and changing your habits.

Invest in yourself. Spend as much as possible on books, audio and video materials, trainings and conferences. Identify your talents and find solutions to monetize them.

A good money management system will provide you solutions to finance your growth and supports your transformation into the super engine that your financial success vehicle needs.

"An investment in knowledge pays the best interest."

Benjamin Franklin (1706-1790)

3. Money management is about investing

"In investing, what is comfortable is rarely profitable."

Robert D. Arnott (1954 -)

Money management is about changing your focus from spending to investing. It may seem quite a challenge. This is where money management comes to help you.

At times, you will have to stretch and step out of your comfort zone. You may be forced to reduce your personal money and recreation and entertainment budget in order to achieve your goals. When you face these types of situations always ask yourself: what is my long term benefit from doing this expenditure? If the answer is none or it is not aligned with your financial goals, probably you will need to think twice if you want to do it or not.

Know the limits of your comfort zone and exercise stepping out of it inch by inch every day. You may start by redirecting 1% more from your income to savings or personal investments every quarter. The best opportunity may be missed when you are not used to stretch to reach it.

"Know what you own, and know why you own it."

Peter Lynch (1944 -)

Do your research before taking a decision. You will need some effort and knowledge to do it. Investing is more than stocks,

Money Management

bonds, real estate, or money and capital market instruments. Investing is any kind of purchase that will bring back a return on the long run. Training and educating yourself continuously is an investment. Creating and maintaining good relationships with your partners are investments. Healthy food and healthy lifestyle is one of the most important investments.

Start investing! Money management will help you find solutions to reroute your cash-flow from spending to investing.

4. Money management is a lifestyle.

"It's not how much money you make, but how much money you keep, how hard it works for you, and how many generations you keep it for."

Robert Kiyosaki (1947 -)

There are a lot of studies in different countries about the lottery winners. Did you know that in every country most of the big lottery winners are back to their initial financial status within years' time? In some cases we discuss tens of millions of dollars.

How come?

Regardless of your financial situation, you should be focused on actively managing your money. Money management is about a lifestyle. It is about constant awareness about your financial status and your financial evolution.

Money management will support you in creating and developing the habits and mindset not only to create your financial success but more important to maintain it for the rest of your life.

"We are what we repeatedly do. Excellence, then, is not an act but a habit."

Aristotle (384 BC – 322 BC)

Now it is the time for action. Start practicing these simple things every day and soon enough you'll start noticing how your financial situation and your entire life will change for better.

"It's not knowing what to do, it's doing what you know."

Anthony Robbins (1960 -)

ABOUT THE AUTHOR

Senol Asan is a successful retail banking expert with more than 12 years of experience in retail banking and more than 7 years of management and leadership positions within the most important financial group of Romania.

He is Supervisory Board member to one of the top life insurance companies in his country. He held advisory positions to both financial and retail Board Members of the biggest bank in the country.

Senol is an expert on leadership, communication, negotiations, sales and sales management, business development and project management, and performance management. He had public speaking engagements on leadership in different countries in Central and Eastern Europe.

Senol has participated in trainings with some of the most important international trainers from USA, Canada, UK, France, Spain, Austria, Slovenia and Romania.

Senol is the founder of AlterHabit Institute which provides personal and leadership development programs. For more information contact: alterhabit.institute@gmail.com.

www.ingramcontent.com/pod-product-compliance
Lightning Source LLC
Chambersburg PA
CBHW051330170526
45166CB00002B/760